Dear Meagan,

Merry Texan Christmas! I hope you know that you are always welcome in Texas or wherever in the world I may be. Until you find a cowboy of your own I thought you might enjoy reading about 'em. Hope you enjoy the book.

Love,
Erin

christmas 2002

COWBOY

[THE LEGEND AND THE LEGACY]

COWBOY

[THE LEGEND AND THE LEGACY]

TEXT BY B.A. PAYTON

PHOTOGRAPHS BY GARY FIEGEHEN

DESIGN BY JIM SKIPP

GREYSTONE BOOKS

DOUGLAS & McINTYRE PUBLISHING GROUP

VANCOUVER / TORONTO / NEW YORK

Acknowledgments

The authors wish to thank the following people for their help, encouragement, advice, and enthusiasm:
Liz, Bronc, Willee, and Jesse Twan; Doug and Marie Mervyn; Lily Harned; Sara Whitney; Mary and Lee Skipp;
Lucy Kenward; Rob Sanders; Mark Denny of Cariboo Saddlery; Kevin Taylor of Hollywood Cowboys;
David Longworth, cowboy poet; Monty Bassett, rodeo clown; Evelyn Maurice; Myra and Sophie Reidemann;
Michael Downs; Brad Thomas; Michael Guy; Frank Palmer; the Williams Lake Stampede; Grant Huffman;
Evan and Linda Lou Howarth and Terje Ness of the Cotton Ranch; Larry Ramstad of the Gang Ranch;
J.Rosettis; and all the cowboys and cowgirls of the Alkali Lake Ranch past and present.

00 01 02 03 04   5 4 3 2 1

Greystone Books
A division of Douglas & McIntyre Ltd.
2323 Quebec Street, Suite 201
Vancouver, British Columbia V5T 4S7

CANADIAN CATALOGUING IN PUBLICATION DATA

Payton, B. A., 1966-
  Cowboy

Includes bibliographical references.
ISBN 1-55054-544-2
  1. Cowboys—West (U.S.) 2. Cowboys—West (U.S.)—Pictorial works. I. Fiegehen, Gary, 1947- II. Title.
F596.P39 2000   636.2'13'092278   C99-911126-4

Library of Congress Cataloguing-in-Publication Data available upon request.

Edited by Lucy Kenward
Design by Jim Skipp
Front cover photograph courtesy of Twan Archives
Back cover photograph by Gary Fiegehen
Typeset by Michael Guy
Printed and bound in Hong Kong
Printed on acid-free paper ∞

The publisher gratefully acknowledges the support of the Canada Council for the Arts and of the British
Columbia Ministry of Tourism, Small Business and Culture. The publisher also acknowledges the financial
support of the Government of Canada through the Book Publishing Industry Development Program (BPIDP)
for its publishing activities..

Previous page: In the Old West, most cowboys were just past boyhood—typically in their teens and early twenties.

Contents

A Man Suited to His Times

(There is) something romantic about him. He lives on horseback as do Bedouins; he fights on horseback, as did the knights of chivalry; he goes armed with a strange new weapon which he uses ambidextrously and precisely; he swears like a trooper, drinks like a fish, wears clothes like an actor, and fights like a devil. He's gracious to ladies, reserved toward strangers, generous to his friends, and brutal to his enemies. He is a cowboy. . . .

—Walter Prescott Webb

A Man Suited to His Times

Below: *The cowboy's open range: a wild and unforgiving land of opportunity.*

Facing page: *Native Americans helped establish the North American cattle industry in the late 1700s and have been working as cowboys ever since.*

There is no more enduring icon of the American West than the cowboy. Embodying the virtues of honesty, integrity, and rugged independence, the cowboy was a new breed of man invented for a new kind of life in a vast, untamed wilderness. From motion pictures to fashion, literature to advertising, we celebrate the romance and adventure of the cowboy's life—a life lived large on the wide-open range.

At the heart of this legend is a simple man; a young, poorly paid migrant worker shifting stock from one lonely place to another. His work was dangerous, backbreaking, and dirty, and his sweat helped make other men rich. Yet despite his hard life and meager means, we hold him in high esteem. Among America's greatest folk heroes, the cowboy has no peer.

His story begins way out west, clear on the far side of the continent. The early ranches of Spanish California were the birthplace of the North American cattle trade and the horsemen who made it pay. The cowboy, that quintessential American idol, was actually a Spanish/Indian invention developed long before the gringo ruled the range.

When Franciscan missionaries began arriving in California in 1769, they brought with them small herds of domestic cattle. As their herds thrived on the rich, wild grass, the fathers soon found themselves in need of assistance. Indian "neophytes" (a euphemism for willing slaves) were the only hands available. They were taught horsemanship, roping, roundup, cutting, and branding, and then they gradually made these skills their own. These vaqueros (from the Spanish *vaca*, meaning cow), developed a unique pastoral society that would later give rise to American cattle culture.

After the United States went to war with Mexico in 1846, and annexed California in 1848, the vaqueros' days north of the Rio Grande and the Gila River soon came to an end. In the newly seized territory, the Americans rushed into the cattle business and quickly replaced the vaqueros (pronounced "ba-care-rows") with their own "buckaroos."

These new cowboys were a cross-section of a society on the move. In the aftermath of the U.S. Civil War, the cowboys' ranks swelled with southern gentlemen whose estates had been ravaged, newly freed slaves yearning to become their own masters, eastern farm boys looking for excitement, refugees searching desperately for work, and criminals trying to stay just beyond the reach of the law. Nearly one in three were either Mexican or Black. Although the white majority of cowboys—like other men of their time—were unrepentant racists, they all somehow managed to work together, develop an industry, and become fabled horsemen in a wild and unforgiving land.

In the imaginations of people living east of the ninety-eighth meridian, whose knowledge of the West came mostly from dime novels, the cowboys' country was "the Great American Desert"—a parched inland sea of shifting sand and bone-bleaching sun, a worthless area fit only for wild beasts and savages. What the Easterners didn't see in their mind's eye was the grass. Millions of acres of rich green and dry golden blades, all of it attractive to cattle, blanketed what came to be known as the Great Plains.

As cattle flourished on the natural bounty, land developers and

Facing page: Although real-life cowboys were just hired hands, the success of dime-novel westerns helped elevate them to celebrity status. Being well aware of their public image, cowboys quickly learned how to strike a winning pose for photographers roaming the range.

Below: *To survive this unforgiving land, a cowboy's packhorse saddle had to carry all the necessities of life.*

Previous page: *Nevada Desert. The striking vistas and open skies of the cowboy's range made dramatic backdrops for Hollywood directors.*

Below: *Tin sheriff's badge. For generations, "Cowboys and Indians" was a popular children's game in countless backyards and vacant lots across the land.*

traders in the east plotted to open up the West, and the tracks of the Union Pacific and Central Pacific railways snaked their way across the range. The iron horse transported cattle to hungry markets back east, and helped develop an urban appetite for longhorn beef. But just as surely as the locomotive's whistle heralded the cowboy's golden age, it also marked the beginning of the end for the open range that made him.

In addition to longhorn cattle, growing herds of sheep grazed the plains ever more heavily and a range war flared up between homesteaders, sheep ranchers, and cattlemen. What was once seen as an endless wasteland became a hotly contested, overtaxed resource. In the rush for profits, the vast sea of grass was damaged almost beyond recovery. Cattle starved and their owners went bankrupt; bad weather sent the booming market into a tailspin. Then, in 1874, Joseph F. Glidden introduced his patented barbed wire fencing material to the open range; it changed the land forever.

Barbed wire, or the Devil's rope as the Indians called it, allowed

They say that Heaven is a free range land

Good-by, Good-by, O fare you well;

But it's barbed wire fence for the Devil's hat band

And barbed wire down in Hell!

—Old cowboy song

settlers to fence off land from the great herds of cattle and made farming possible. When the best land, routes, and water sources were all blocked off, cowboys and cattlemen began cutting fences. But barbed wire was cheap and relatively easy to mend, and the farmers stood their ground. Eventually, the cattle barons saw that the open range was lost. They also realized that although barbed wire was effective at keeping cattle out, it could be just as useful for keeping cattle in. Barbed wire made selective breeding possible and transformed the range-cattle industry into a stock-farming business.

With fewer hands needed to tend the same number of cattle, many former cowboys found themselves looking for any work that could preserve a measure of the independence they once knew under the boundless sky. Some took jobs as bartenders, others became prospectors, and a few got work with the Wild West shows. Their cowboyin' years left them ill prepared for jobs in the new economy.

The cowboys' heyday lasted only a few decades, from the end of the

ROY ROGERS

[hats]

A cowboy spent the bulk of his wardrobe budget on his most personal possession, his hat. Sometimes he'd spend a season's wages on a single fancy lid to protect his head from the sun, snow, and low branches. It served as a bucket, basket, and bowl and, of course, made his most important fashion statement. The size, shape, and style of a cowboy's hat gave away his home territory long before anyone got close enough to ask.

Descended from the Spanish-Mexican sombrero, the American cowboy hat came in four distinct styles: the sugar-loaf sombrero (broad brim and high peak), the Montana peak (four-sided crown), the Plainsman (low crown), and the Texas (high crown with a star pinned to the side for the Lone Star State). Today, many cowboys wear a cool, straw hat in summer and a warm, dark felt in winter.

Civil War to the end of the nineteenth century. During that time, over ten million head of cattle were moved from Texas to the railheads in Kansas and Missouri. And yet, at their zenith, cowboys numbered no more than forty thousand. How did they manage to make such an enormous impact on the American psyche?

In the summer of 1893, historian Frederick Jackson Turner delivered his landmark thesis "The Significance of the Frontier in American History" to the American Historical Association. An ideological offspring of the concept of manifest destiny (the idea that God intended the United States to expand to the Pacific Coast), Turner's theory maintained that it was the wild, promising wilderness of the West—not the heritage of Europe—that exerted the single most powerful influence on the forma-tion of American culture. The cowboy seemed to be at the vanguard of this new American identity.

With the help of men like Turner, the cowboy was quickly acclaimed as the American archetype. Big boots to fill—was the cowboy up to the task? Writer Emerson Hough articulated his generation's answer in the *Story of the Cowboy:*

> The cowboy was simply a part of the West. He who did not understand the one could never understand the other.... If we care truly to see the cowboy as he was . . . the first intention should be to study the cowboy in connection with his surroundings. Then perhaps we may not fail in our purpose, but come near to seeing him as he actually was, the product of primitive, chaotic, elemental forces, rough, barbarous, and strong. Then we shall love him because at heart each of us is a barbarian, too, and longing for that past the ictus of whose heredity we can never eliminate from out our blood....And this is the way we should look at the cowboy of the passing West; not as a curiosity, but as a product; not as an eccentric driver of horned cattle, but as a man suited to his times.

Facing page: *The bit, a metal bar placed inside the mouth of a horse, was attached to the headstall and reins and was used to break and, ultimately, guide a horse. After the first few days of training, a good horse responded to the feel of the reins against its neck in order to avoid having the bit pulled against the roof of its mouth.*

Below: *During the cowboy's heyday, longhorn cattle ruled the range. It wasn't until after 1900 that stockier and more profitable British breed cattle replaced them.*

And so an icon was born—one tailor-made for starring roles in movies, novels, radio, television, and advertising. After more than a century of mythmaking, history seems determined to remember the cowboy as a maverick blend of fact and fiction.

Right: *During the era of the silent film, the brightest star in the western skies was Thomas Edwin Mix. Famous for heart-stopping stunts and flashy garb, Mix also directed his own films and never, ever let the facts of the cowboy's life get in the way of a good movie.*

Facing page: *A good horse and a strong rope—how the West was won.*

Following page: *William F. Cody, a.k.a. Buffalo Bill, became one of the chief mythmakers of the Old West. He brought his skills as a hunter, tracker, and Indian fighter to the arena and became a fabulously successful showman. "Buffalo Bill's Wild West" first hit the road in 1883 and toured throughout the U.S. and Europe. Cody's Wild West show offered three full hours of action, including galloping horses, stampeding buffalo, sharpshooting, trick riding, and bronc busting.*

Beasts of
Burden

. . . The irons are hot,
A slick un's caught and taken to the fire,
A cowboy and his trusty steed
Are earning well their hire.

—Dick Gibford,
"The Last Buckaroo"

Beasts of Burden

«**A** cowboy on foot is about as useful as tits on a bull," or so the saying goes. Without a horse, rounding up, branding, and driving cattle from one place to another would have been impossible. What's worse, finding oneself alone and without a horse on the wild, open range was analogous to being tossed overboard at sea. Consequently, horse theft was a serious matter, usually punishable by hanging.

Below: A good horse was controlled as much by a gentle tap with the spurs as by the pull of the reins.

Facing page: The dependable, dispensable tool of the open range has become something more in modern times. Horses, especially wild mustangs, have become a symbol of the vanishing West.

Before a man could become a cowboy, he first had to become a horseman. In the Old West, cowboys rode wild mustangs (from the Spanish *mesteño*, meaning stray), or mustangs interbred with U.S. Calvary stock or eastern work horses. The horses were small: 12–14 hands high (48–56 inches or 122–142 centimeters) and 700–900 pounds (320–410 kilograms). In comparison, today's horses average 14–16 hands (56–64 inches or 142–162 centimeters) and over 1000 pounds (450 kilograms).

The horse was the cowboy's most important tool, but only once it had been broken. In the Old West, bronc busting (taming wild horses) was a full-time specialty for cowboys known as mustangers or bronc busters.

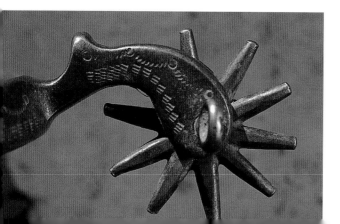

Some men accomplished the job in a single day; others spent up to a week easing the horse into submission. Either way, breaking horses was dangerous work that required a skilled hand, reliable equipment, and a wagonload of patience. But not every skill could be taught. A cutting horse, the most valuable kind, was born with an innate talent for isolating a cow from the herd.

Hollywood portrayals aside, the true nature of the relationship between the cowboy and his horse was surprisingly unsentimental. In the Old West, a cowboy's horse was usually supplied by the outfit he worked for, and he gave the animal just enough care to keep it alive and working. If a cowboy happened to own his horse, he usually put it in with the ranch's common stock as a token of his commitment to the boss. He treated it as a tool and usually worked it into the ground after seven or eight years. Occasionally, if there was no other way to complete a crucial job on time, horses were even ridden to death. Sometimes a horse would return the favor. The most common cause of death for a cowboy was not

[branding irons]

A branding iron was a rod about two or three feet (up to a meter) long with an iron stamp at one end. A rancher's claim to ownership, as well as a community legacy, lay in the brand. A custom dating back over 4000 years to Egypt, branding was brought to the North American cattle industry by the Spanish. Designed to discourage easy alteration, brands were traditionally inspired by the owner's name or some local geographic feature. In addition to having a brand burned into its hide, the animal usually had its ears clipped in a distinctive way in order to identify it over long stretches of open range.

A branding iron had to be extremely hot in order to sear cowhide quickly and cleanly. Nowadays, propane fires are commonly used for branding.

a shootout with Indians or a barroom brawl but being caught up in his own rope or stirrup and being dragged behind his horse.

Although the celebrated love affair between the cowboy and his horse was mostly the stuff of legend, the horse has always defined the cowboy's identity. No self-respecting buckaroo would be caught dead walking anywhere that he could ride.

The other animal that defined the cowboy's life was, of course, the cow. And in the Old West, the cow was always a longhorn. Bred and tended by the Moors for over a thousand years on the plains of North Africa and southern Spain, the first longhorn cattle arrived in the New World at Santo Domingo on Christopher Columbus's second voyage. During the sixteenth and seventeenth centuries, they entered the American heartland from New Spain (Mexico) through Texas and prospered on the open range. By 1886, more than 16.5 million head of cattle roamed between Texas, Kansas, Montana, New Mexico, and Colorado. It was the cowboy's job to get this beef to market.

Right: *The Hollywood treatment. The first true western movie was* The Great Train Robbery *in 1898. For the better part of the twentieth century, mostly B-grade "horse operas" or "oaters" helped transform the cowboy into a larger-than-life icon. Over the years, critics have announced the death of the big-screen western time and time again. However, when we least expect it, the Hollywood cowboy picks himself up, climbs back in the saddle, and hits the trail again.*

Facing page: *Detail of saddle fender on trophy saddle. Rodeo competitions kept the cowboy's skills sharp for the open range.*

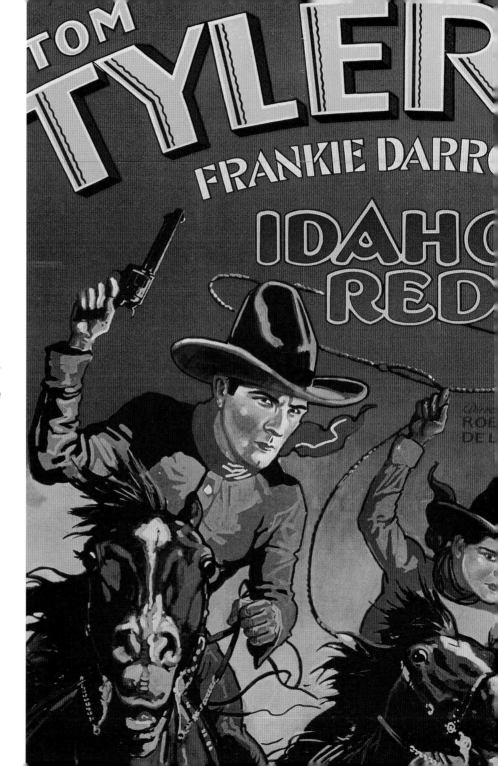

It all began with the round up. Twice a year, in the spring and in the fall, a team of riders would spend days searching the range for widely scattered cattle. The animals were flushed from the scrub, chased across arroyos, and sent splashing through rivers and streams. Sometimes, cowboys would cross hundreds of miles to round up a single herd.

On a typical roundup day, a team of riders would fan out behind a moving chuckwagon and herd the cattle in line behind it. By the afternoon, the chuckwagon would stop and, as their meal was being prepared, the cowboys would ride out in front of the growing herd and close the circle around the wagon and dinner.

On the southern range, cowboys used the spring roundup to brand new calves and to gather mature stock for the drive to market. The fall roundup caught any mature cattle missed in the spring. In the northern territories, cattle were branded and strays collected during the spring, and mature stock was gathered in the fall.

On the open range, where cattle were free to roam, keeping track of

Now Buster Jig was a riata man

With his gut-line coiled up neat,

So he shaken her out an' he built him a loop

An' he lassed the Devil's hind feet.

—Gail Garner,
"The Sierry Petes"

[rope]

The worth of a cowboy was essentially measured by two things: his skill as a horseman and his talent with a rope. A cowboy's rope was the multipurpose extension of his hand, arm, and back. Used to catch horses and cattle—as well as to haul, pull, and tie just about anything else—the cowboy's rope was even occasionally used around a horse rustler's neck. In the Old West, this simple tool went by many names. Although southwestern cowboys called it "rope," cowboys from the Pacific coast preferred the term "lasso," (from the Portuguese word *laco,* meaning snare). It was also widely referred to as a "lariat," a corruption of the Spanish *reata,* meaning "rope to tie horses in single file."

stock was a full-time concern, and branding was the most effective way of proving title. An unbranded cow, or maverick, was fair game for rustlers. The word "maverick" itself contains a warning; it is the legacy of one Sam Maverick, a cattleman from the banks of the San Antonio River whose name lives on in infamy. Sam neglected to brand his stock and found out the hard way that unmarked cattle belong to the first man to heat up an iron. His ranching days were short and not so sweet.

A rustler would usually carry a length of telegraph wire. Inconspicuous and easily concealed, telegraph wire could be bent and shaped to mimic any brand. It could be heated and burned over an old brand so seamlessly that it was nearly impossible to distinguish the altered marking from the original. Other times a rustler "cold branded" his boss's cattle with light, impermanent marks that would quickly heal over and could soon be replaced by a different brand.

When a cattle rustler was caught, the offended party usually dispensed swift, often lethal retribution. Frontier society viewed the protection of

Below: Cowboy trading cards, popular in the early 1900s, often dramatized and romanticized frontier justice.

Facing page: A cowboy didn't ordinarily carry a rifle while tending cattle, but when he did, it was usually the celebrated Winchester repeating rifle, often referred to as "the gun that won the West." More often, he carried a handgun in a saddlebag or a holster.

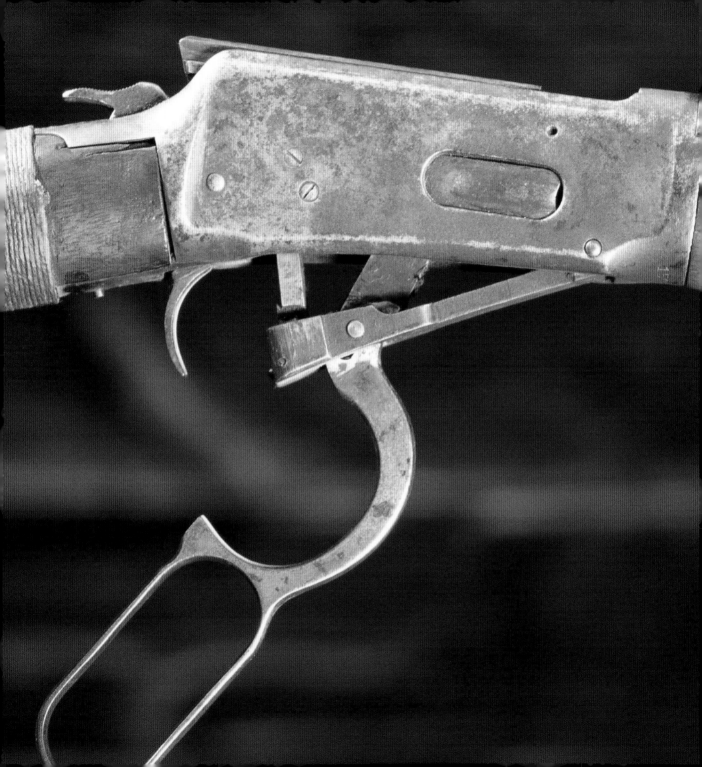

Facing page: *The cowboy's boots: born of necessity, built to stand the test of time.*

Left: *Like Superman and Batman, the comic-book cowboy often possessed superhuman skills and strength.*

property by any means as righteous and necessary. But in the main, this rule applied (as so often rules do) only to the small-time rustler. When a neighboring cattle baron pinched a few cows from his rival, it was usually met with tolerance and a blind eye turned.

During roundup and branding time, cowboys gathered socially as well as on the job. Old friends (and rivals) boasted about who among them was the best all-around cowboy. In the late afternoon, when the work was done, the men amused themselves with contests of horsemanship and general horsing around. These celebrations—stretching back to the original vaquero—have always attracted the fastest, the toughest, and those with something to prove.

Vaqueros called the roundup and its accompanying celebrations "rodeo" (from the Spanish *rodear,* meaning to surround or encircle). American buckaroos, however, distinguished between the rodeo and the roundup, using the word "rodeo" to describe the contest of cowboy skills.

Among the events, one popular with vaqueros in old California—and

[saddles]

Because the open-range cowboy made his living sitting down on the job, his saddle was his most valuable piece of gear. In the Old West, a cowboy's horse usually belonged to his boss, but his saddle was his own property. The cowboy's saddle bore the marks of hard work and was often embellished with cantle rims, silver conchas (fancy shell-shaped ornaments), and engravings. A well-maintained saddle lasted as long as thirty years and often became a family heirloom.

Today's western saddle is designed for the North American range, and, although the style has evolved over the years, it is a direct descendant of the sixteenth-century Spanish war saddle that was first ridden into North America by the conquistadors. In the Old West, a good custom saddle weighed 40–50 pounds (18–23 kilograms) and took about six weeks to construct. It consisted of leather laid over a wooden frame or "tree," a cantle, or curved back of the seat, and a horn at the front for roping and dragging.

later with their American counterparts—involved burying a chicken up to its neck in the sand, riding by at full gallop, then bending over to pull it up like a turnip. Roping grizzlies was all the rage in those early days, but eventually, calf roping and bronc- and bull-riding competitions established themselves as perennial rodeo favorites.

Acrobatics on horseback were always a popular cowboy pastime, but it wasn't until 1893 that the stunt riding we've come to expect of modern rodeo was found in the cowboy's bag of tricks. That year, the Chicago World's Columbian Exposition hosted Russian Cossacks who performed show-stopping stunts on horseback in front of stunned audiences. News traveled fast. The American cowboy quickly purloined the Russian moves and gave them a dash of western derring-do. Within a generation, the tricks became rodeo standards—and rodeo became a national pastime.

King of the Rodeo, but that's a young man's game

It's good to feel a bucking bronc, have someone call your name.

But my rodeo days are over, I ride the rough one for my pay

King of the Rodeo, but that just lasts a day. . . .

—Robert Strader,
"King of the Rodeo"

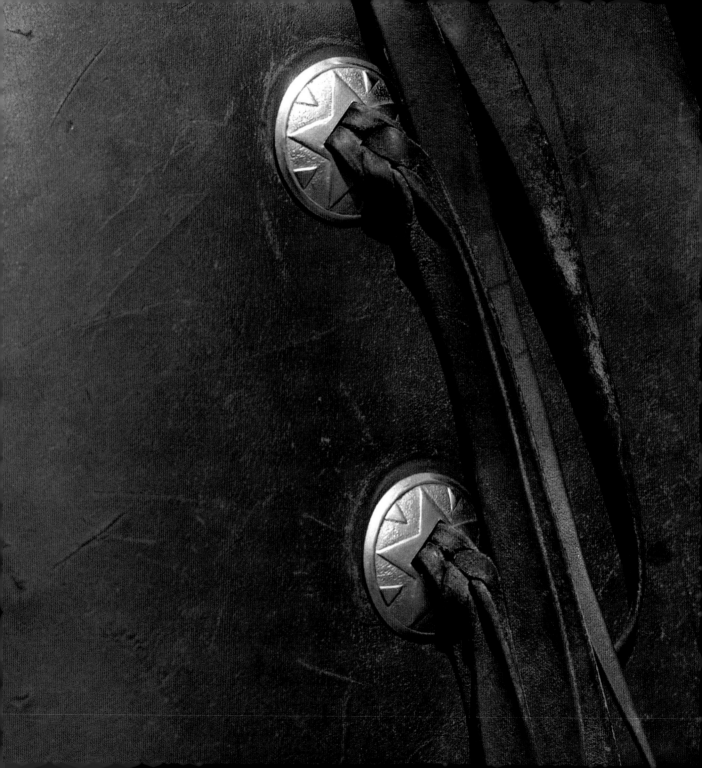

The Cattle Drives

Ho, I'm a jolly cowboy,

from Texas now I hail;

Give me my quirt and pony,

I'm ready for the trail;

I love the rolling prairies,

they're free from care and strife,

Behind a herd of longhorns,

I'll journey all my life.

—N. Howard Thorpe,
"Songs of the Cowboys"

The Cattle Drives

West of the ninety-eighth meridian, the eastern forests thinned and gave way to rolling waves of grass with names like gramma, buffalo, bluestem, pleurisy roo, sand droopseed, and bluejoint turkeyfoot to name a few. Before the coming of Europeans, the Great Plains—which stretched from the Rocky Mountains to the Mississippi River, and from Saskatchewan to the heart of Texas—supported perhaps as many as seventy-five million bison.

In the post–Civil War years, however, the bison (or buffalo as they were commonly known) were slaughtered for their hides, for industry, and for target practice. The railway companies made fortunes transporting their bones back to eastern processing centers to be pulverized and transformed into carbon, bone china, and fertilizer. The buffalo's demise spelled starvation and the end of a way of life for many Plains Indians. It also resulted in a newly vacant sea of grass.

Enter the longhorn. Across this open land of rolling hills, sheer canyons, and flat, arid wastelands, longhorn cattle quickly reclaimed the

Right: *The crack of a bullwhip was often enough to urge cattle in the right direction.*

Facing page: *Typical trail cuisine didn't spare the calories, cholesterol, fat, or caffeine.*

buffalo's historic range. But unlike the Indians who took only what they could eat, the cowboys rounded up enormous herds and pushed them toward the railway.

Following trails with names like Chisholm, Western, Shawnee, and Goodnight-Loving, cattle drives would last three to four months and cover hundreds of miles through merciless sun or driving wind and rain. During that time, the cowboy relied solely on his horse, his lariat, and the men by his side. Longhorn cattle were about as wild and unpredictable as the land they grazed, yet rounding up a herd of up to several thousand animals took a surprisingly small team of skilled men and horses.

The head of the crew was the trail boss. He took full responsibility for the success of the enterprise and, like a ship's captain out on the high seas, his word was law. The crew also had a wrangler who took care of the remuda, the herd of spare horses, and acted as a general gofer for the trail boss and the cook. Everyone tried to stay in the good graces of the cook, as he held considerable power to make or break crew morale. Though

Jim don't go in for purple chaps,

Nor poker, booze and song,

A steady chap whom people trust,

A lad who don't go wrong. . . .

—Floyd T. Wood,
"My Puncher Man"

[chaps]

Chaps (pronounced "shaps," and from the Spanish *chaparejos,* meaning leather breeches or overalls) were leather leg aprons that protected the thighs and knees from brush, barbed wire, burrs, rope burn, biting horses, and snakes. The most common styles in the Old West were the early tight-fitting shotguns, which were long and straight like the barrels of a shotgun, then the widely popular wraparound batwings, and in cold northern territories, fur-covered woollies.

surrounded by cattle, the cook rarely served beef because too much of the animal would spoil in the sweltering conditions; pork 'n' beans, biscuits, and strong coffee, however, were made available in copious amounts. The cowboys were left to concentrate on keeping the herd together, calm, and moving toward the railway.

To escape the searing heat of the midday sun, the cowboy was up and moving before dawn. Following the cows and the lead bulls through choking clouds of dust, he settled into the clicking rhythm of the cattle's ankle joints, the dull thud of hooves, and the sharp clatter of horns. Sometimes, a cowboy's biggest challenge was just to stay awake and in the saddle. He'd rub tobacco juice in his eyes to make up for little or no sleep. Other times, when the lead cows were spooked by rattlesnakes or wolves, a stampede would break the monotony. Charging cows were known to split around a fallen rider; still a cowboy did everything in his power to avoid putting this theory to the test.

Outside the pages of dime novels, relations between cowboys and

Facing Page: The cowboy's penchant for turning simple bridles and bits into "horse jewelry" helped elevate his gear from basic tack into functional art, which has become highly prized by collectors.

Below: *In addition to heating up irons, branding fires were often used for boiling black coffee and frying up a meal of fresh prairie oysters (calf testicles).*

Right: *Buffalo Bill made a fortune reenacting battles between settlers and Indians. For authenticity, his Wild West extravaganza even employed the likes of Sitting Bull, the Sioux chief who oversaw the demise of General George Armstrong Custer at Little Big Horn in 1876.*

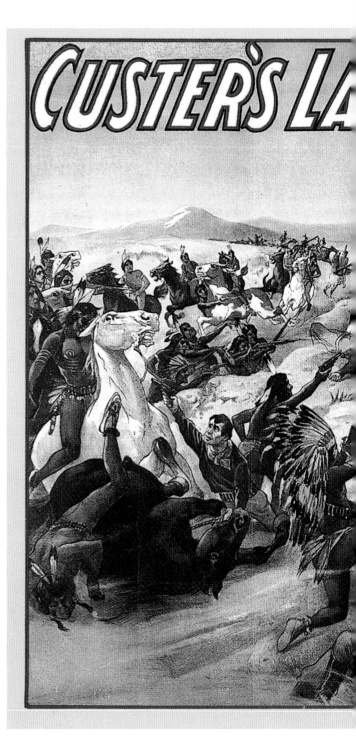

AS PRESENTED BY

STAND BUFFALO BILL'S
WILD WEST.

Below and facing page: Maker's marks. Early saddle makers, producing handmade saddles in the distinctive styles of various territories, practiced their craft all over the West. Makers often proudly featured their marks on the back of the cantle rim.

Indians on the open range mostly involved cowboys paying a toll to cross Indian land. The Indians aimed to collect in cash, horses, or cattle, and they extracted their tribute by whatever means necessary, including threat, begging, or theft. The extermination of the buffalo, the wars with invading "pioneers," and being forced into close quarters with old enemies on marginal land all contributed to the Indians' suffering. The cattle passing their way represented a much-needed source of food. In order to avoid any trouble, trail bosses usually offered the Indians a few cows up front, and considered it just another cost of doing business.

Out under the stars, with little more than a soogan (quilt) between him and the land, the cowboy rarely got a decent sleep. Sometimes, the mosquitoes were so thick that a man would suffocate under his tarp while trying to escape the ravenous plague. And then there were the storms. After the first downpour, the cowboy would have to sleep in soaked blankets for several nights to come. If the weather was good and the bugs left him alone, the cowboy could get a couple of hours rest. He would doze off

despite the snoring of his comrades, the lowing of the cattle, and the occasional snort of his horse—then get up early and start the routine all over again.

At the end of the trail, the cowboy used a long prod to force cows up a chute and into the waiting rail cars. Because of this tedious chore, the men referred to each other as cowpokes or cattle punchers. When the job was done, and the cows were on their way to market, the cowboy would collect about a hundred dollars for his trouble—barely enough money for a new hat and a good set of boots.

Below: *While Buck Jones never made it to the White House, the nation wouldn't have to wait too long until Ronald Reagan, a fellow Hollywood cowboy, rode into the highest office in the land.*

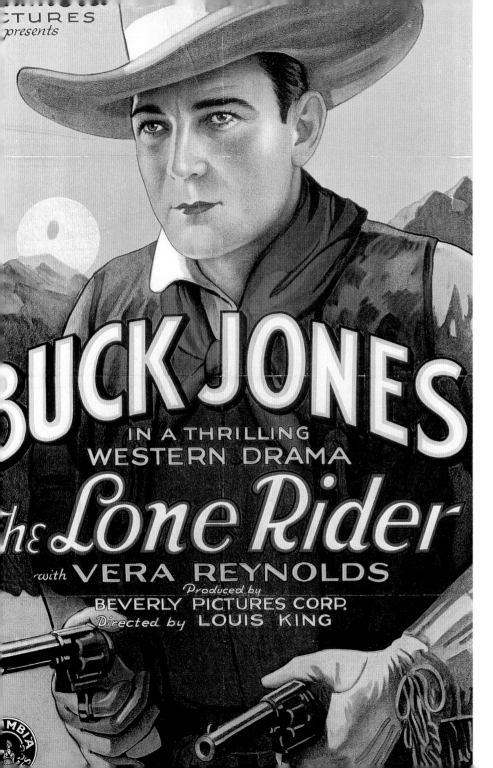

BUCK JONES

IN A THRILLING
WESTERN DRAMA

The Lone Rider

with VERA REYNOLDS

Produced by
BEVERLY PICTURES CORP.
Directed by LOUIS KING

Left: *The image of the lone outsider was central to Hollywood's portrayal of the cowboy.*

Following page: *Tough, warm, and impervious to wind, buckskin jackets were worn to work in the cooler months.*

Come along, boys, and listen to my tale;
I'll tell you of my troubles on the old Chisholm Trail.

Come a ti yi yippy, yippy yea, yippy yea,
Come a ti yi yippy, yippy yea. . . .

I popped my foot in the stirrup and gave a little yell;
The trail cattle broke and the leaders went to hell.

You strap on your chaps, your spurs and your gun—
You're going into town to have a little fun.

You play with a gambler who's got a marked pack;
You walk back to camp with your saddle on your back.

Singin' hi yi yippy, hi yippy yea,
Singin' hi yi yippy, yippy yea yea.

—**"The Old Chisholm Trail"**

Trail's End

. . . *so I headed for a place across the street, where I could hear a fiddle. It was a saloon, gambling and dance hall. Here I saw an old long-haired fellow dealing monte. I went to the bar and called for a toddy, and as I was drinking it a girl came up and put her little hand under my chin, and looked me square in the face and said 'Oh you pretty Texas boy, give me a drink.'* . . .

—J. L. McCaleb,
The Trail Drivers of Texas

Trail's End

Facing page: *Dime-novel dandies. Before the dust had settled on the Civil War, an army of hack writers set about writing dime novels of an imaginary West that most of them had never seen. For the most part, they created a melodramatic world peopled with glib stock characters—many of which became permanent fixtures in cowboy legend.*

When they were away from home, particularly at the end of a cattle drive, cowboys congregated in cowtowns: Newton, Ellsworth, Wichita, Caldwell, and Dodge City among them. The first, Abilene, got its start in 1867, and for four years it was the undisputed cowboy capital of the world. Although it was eclipsed by newer and bigger centers, Abilene remained the prototype and would be remembered fondly as the granddaddy of them all. The most successful cowtowns were located in Kansas, and they were all designed to take full advantage of a single resource— cowboys on the loose.

Contrary to innumerable dime-novel plots, the average cowboy did not ride into town whooping it up and shooting everything in sight. Typically, he arrived exhausted after having spent between one and four months in the saddle. He had worked and slept in the same clothes every day, his boots were worn out, his hat caked with sweat and mud, and he was well tired of staring at the scruffy mugs of his fellow riders. After a season of choking on dust and chafing under the pressure of never-

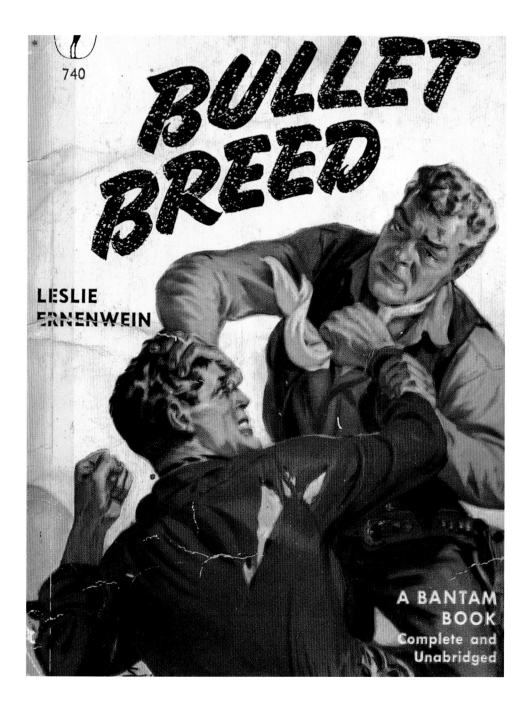

740

BULLET BREED

LESLIE ERNENWEIN

A BANTAM
BOOK
Complete and
Unabridged

Below: *Wells Fargo. All the hard-earned cash collected from cowboys needed protection from unsavory elements. Wells Fargo agents escorted wagonloads of loot out of cowtowns to more secure locations.*

Facing page: *At the tail end of a cattle drive, cowboys were ready to scare up some fun. After a few drinks, however, some cowpokes couldn't tell whether they were coming or going.*

ending work, it was little wonder that he was ready to blow off some steam. And, with a small wad of cash burning a hole in his pocket, he could well afford some fun.

A cowtown, no matter how humble, was like an oasis in a vast desert. As the cowboy rode off the range and into "civilization," he was met by a dusty main street of false-fronted buildings, shop windows crammed with all sorts of merchandise and amusements, and assorted dens of iniquity—all ready and waiting to quickly separate him from his hard-earned wages.

The cowboy's first stop would be at the bathhouse to scrub and shave the filth of the trail from his hide. Next, he might visit the local haberdasher to buy a new set of clothes. From there, he would head straight for the saloon or the whorehouse. Cowtowns were crawling with "soiled doves," "calico queens," and "painted cats"—all euphemisms for women with favors to sell. Despite the carnal temptations, the odd cowboy was content just to dance the night away. Joseph McCoy, of Abilene, described such a night in one of the local saloons:

Below: *Even after the cowtowns faded into history, cowboys never forgot how to celebrate a job well done.*

Facing page: *Guns ablazin'. From comic books and dime novels to radio and television, pop culture often portrayed cowboys as men who shot first and asked questions later.*

The cow-boy enters the dance with a peculiar zest, not stopping to divest himself of his sombrero, spurs, or pistols, but just as he dismounts off his cow-pony, so he goes into the dance. A more odd, not to say comical sight, is not often seen than the dancing cow-boy; with the front of his sombrero lifted at an angle a fully forty-five degrees; his huge spurs jingling at every step or notion; his revolvers slapping up and down like a retreating sheep's tail; his eyes lit up with excitement, liquor and lust; he plunges in and 'hoes it down' at a terrible rate, in the most approved yet awkward country style; often swaying 'his partner' clear off of the floor for an entire circle, and 'balance all' with an occasional demonical yell, near akin to the war whoop of the savage Indian.

While most cowboys concentrated on having a good time in the frontier cowtowns, men like William H. Bonney, a.k.a. Billy the Kid, worked

For down the street there came a-walkin'

My old-time pardner of yore,

And although I know you will not believe me,

Let me tell you what he wore.

He had his boots outside his britches'

They was made of leather, green and red.

His shirt was of a dozen colors,

Loud enough to wake the dead.

—Gail Garner,
"The Dude Wrangler"

[boots]

Cowboy boots—with their underslung heel, laceless, knee-grazing tops, and thin soles for better stirrup feel—evolved in the late 1860s from the low-heeled boots worn by the U.S. Cavalry. Early cowboy boots were designed strictly for riding, and they were completely unsuited for walking. For a custom fit, a cowboy would mail a paper tracing of his foot to the cobbler who would make the boots to order. A good pair of boots could cost upward of two months' wages.

overtime to tarnish the cowboy's reputation. Although Bonney started out as a buckaroo, and a pint-sized one at that, he quickly became a horse thief, a cattle rustler, a murderer, and the ultimate example of the cowboy gone bad. He killed twenty-one men in all, one for each candle on his last birthday cake, and by the time he finally met his Maker—introduction compliments of Sheriff Pat Garrett—the Kid's legend was secure.

Although cowboys were for the most part law abiding, and men like Bonney were the exception to the rule, the buckaroo began parodying his reputation for lawlessness—mugging for portraits with his guns drawn, playing tricks on hapless Easterners, and staging mock hangings for unsuspecting tourists. To the cowboy, it was all in good fun. By 1872, however, the good citizens of Abilene decided that they'd had enough, as the following notice published in the local *Chronicle* unequivocally attests:

> We, the undersigned members of the Farmers Protective Association, and officers and citizens of Dickinson County,

Facing page: *Fancy leatherwork and ornaments dressed up a saddle's cantle rim. A desperate (or inebriated) cowboy might bet his boss's horse in a card game, but never his own saddle.*

Below: *The .44 caliber Colt Army Revolver (1860) was a favorite of cowboys and gunmen on the open range.*

Kansas, most respectfully request all who have contemplated riding Texas cattle to Abilene in the coming season to seek some other point for shipment, as the inhabitants of Dickinson will no longer submit to the evils of the trade.

The cowboys got the message and moved on to other counties. But soon the cowtowns, the cattle drives, and the open range itself were all in sharp decline. The great cattle ranches were redefining the industry, and growing in number and in influence. The barons of these new empires preferred to keep their subjects close at hand. This meant that the cowboy started spending most of his free time at the ranch. As with the open range, the attempt to domesticate the cowboy met with some resistance.

Downwind from the ranch house, and conveniently close to the stable, the cowboy hung his hat. Aptly named and completely utilitarian, his bunkhouse served as a constant reminder that ranches were designed for the comfort and well-being of cows, not of cowboys.

Below: *Detail of chaps. Ranches sometimes provided the more expensive pieces of gear for their modestly paid cowboys.*

Facing page: *The rise of the great ranches gave cattle barons an opportunity to keep a closer eye on their cowboys.*

After stepping through the door, the first thing a visitor would notice was the smell: a pungent potpourri of manure, dirt, chewing tobacco, mesquite or cottonwood smoke, sweaty boots, saddle leather, and a general manly scent. Often, buffalo hides served as doors and wolf skins covered the bunks, as did lice, ticks, and fleas. Occasionally, cowboys would go through the effort of whitewashing the walls or laying wood planks over the dirt floor, but by and large their bunkhouses were notoriously unkempt places for no self-respecting buckaroo took an interest in the "woman's work" of cleaning up after himself. And what would be the point? In the Old West, men outnumbered women ten to one and the chances of bringing a female visitor back to the bunkhouse were very slim indeed.

The cowboy passed his spare time playing cards, dominoes, banjos, and Jew's harps. Bunkhouse reading material consisted mainly of picture magazines, mail-order catalogs, and dime-novel westerns. After passing through the grubby hands of those who could read, used literature often

Below: *This lonesome shack, the remnants of an old line camp, slowly surrenders to the elements.*

ended up papering the walls. Guns were favorite playthings, and indoor target practice was common. Most cowboys were barely past boyhood, typically in their late teens or early twenties, and when cooped up together, they were prone to boredom and mischief. One favorite way to kill time was to haul a fellow cowboy into a hastily convened kangaroo court on a trumped-up charge such as stuttering or bragging. The defendant was always found guilty after his comrades' damning testimony and was summarily sentenced to a humiliating penalty such as getting whacked on the backside with a quirt.

Once or twice a year, the cowboy left the ranch for line camp, the semi-permanent bivouac used when tending cattle on a ranch's far-off range. Most line camps were attended by one or two cowhands and consisted of a single-room shack of sod or logs, or sometimes a small cave gouged into the side of a hill. A few lonely weeks of line-camp duty made the grungy old bunkhouse seem like Home Sweet Home.

Facing page: *One more time with feeling. During their off-hours, cowboys invented homegrown harmonies of the cattle ranch and range.*

Below: *A tool kit fashioned from the top of an old boot. Often strapped to a saddle, such tool kits kept needles, thread, pliers, and other necessities close at hand.*

Right: *Idle hands. Cowboy art made from shoeing nails, on permanent display in a barn.*

Facing page: *Woollies. For cowboys, warm angora goat or sheepskin chaps came with a fringe benefit—their manufacture helped remove a few more "range maggots" from cattle country.*

Following page, left: *Sidesaddle no more. Sometimes, the best man for the job was a cowgirl.*

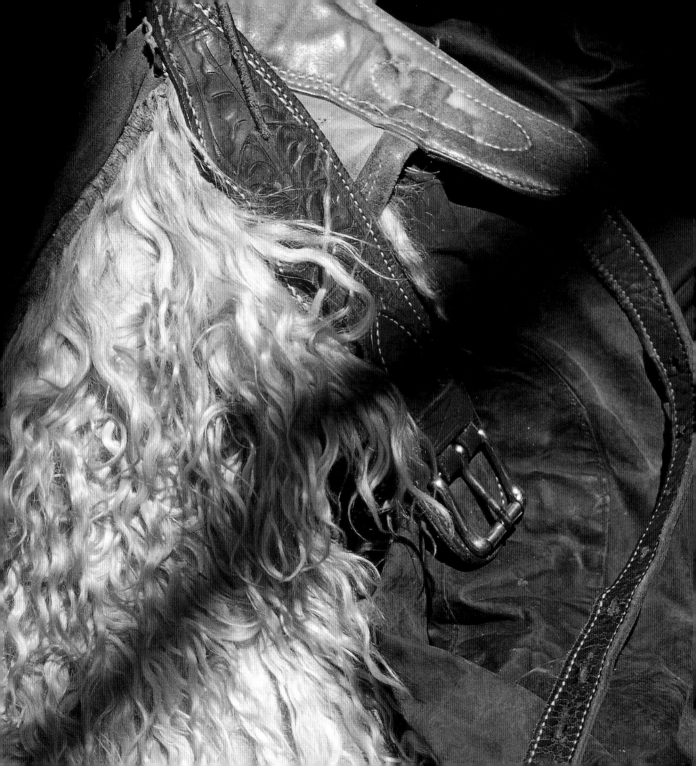

Speaking of your farms and your shanty charms,

Speaking of your silver and gold,

Take a cowman's advice,

Go and marry you a true and lovely little wife,

Never to roam, always stay at home;

That's a cowman's advice,

Way up on the Kansas line.

—from "The Kansas Line,"
A traditional cowboy song

Parting Shots

Mamas don't let your babies grow up to be cowboys.

—Title of the song by Ed and Patsy Bruce

Parting Shots

Below: *Like a well-placed dueling scar on the cheek, a bullet hole in a cowboy's hat was a sought-after mark of distinction. Some were even authentic.*

Facing page: *Scratching the trigger finger on a lazy afternoon.*

The cowboy of the open range is gone but not forgotten. Like the vaquero before him, he has passed the reins to a new generation. On ranches from Texas to British Columbia and California to North Dakota, men (and now women) still rope, brand, and tend cattle. Sometimes they work with all-terrain vehicles and helicopters, other times they just saddle up a horse. Few people can earn a living as honest-to-goodness cowboys in the modern world of fences and scientific stock farming; however, there are plenty of folks who dress the part.

Although the open-range cowboy spent a big chunk of his wages on gear, he was a member of a society in which rank and prestige had little to do with the way a man dressed. He was judged on his skills and his ability to get the job done. Today, though, his gear holds a mystique that goes far beyond simple tack and garb; it has become the national costume. Kids don't dress up as lawyers or salesmen for Halloween; cowboys are the heroes of childhood dreams.

Popular culture has transformed the cowboy into an international

Right: *Hopalong Cassidy was the hero of twenty-eight western novels written by Clarence E. Mulford. Actor William Boyd brought the character to the silver screen, starring as Cassidy in sixty-six motion pictures. For fans the world over, Boyd and Cassidy are synonymous. In addition to appearing in movies, Boyd recreated the character in a popular television show for kids, complete with his own creed promoting model cowboy behavior.*

Hopalong Cassidy's Creed for American Boys & Girls:

- *The highest badge of honor a person can wear is honesty. Be truthful at all times.*

- *Your parents are the best friends you have. Listen to them and obey their instructions.*

- *If you want to be respected, you must respect others. Show good manners in every way.*

- *Only through hard work and study can you succeed. Don't be lazy. Your good deeds always come to light. So don't boast or be a show-off.*

- *If you waste time or money today, you will regret it tomorrow. Practice thrift in all ways.*

- *Many animals are good and loyal companions. Be friendly and kind to them.*

- *A strong, healthy body is a precious gift. Be neat and clean.*

- *Our country's laws are made for your protection. Observe them carefully.*

- *Children in many foreign lands are less fortunate than you. Be glad and proud you are an American.*

I am a wandering cowboy,

From ranch to ranch I roam;

At every ranch when welcome,

I make myself at home.

—John R. Craddock,
"The Wandering Cowboy"

[stirrups]

Stirrups kept the cowboy more comfortable and securely anchored in the saddle by holding his feet against the horse's flank to provide balance and maneuverability while riding. Although they were usually made of wood covered in leather, stirrups made of steel were introduced in the 1890s. Touted as sturdier and easier to produce, the metal version quickly fell out of favor because it conducted cold in the winter and was not as safe as the more flexible wooden variety.

Below: *Moving camp and packing salt for cattle.*

Facing page: *A buckaroo tames a wild pickup truck.*

Following page: *An image to uphold. Cowboyin' was more than just a job, it was a society to which some men aspired.*

star. From Tokyo to Paris, and from Cape Town to New Delhi, the image of a mounted rider with a Stetson instantly conjures up the American buckaroo. And what has his image come to represent? Through the power of the media, the cowboy has been simplified to a stock character that now almost completely eclipses the reality of his life. This new Western icon is independent, courageous, skillful, honest, virile—in short, everything a man should be. From the squeaky-clean singing cowboys of Hollywood fame to honky-tonk buckaroos riding electric bulls across the land, the very concept of the cowboy has undergone dramatic and often ridiculous permutations. He has also quickly become a cash cow. For well over a century, advertisers have been using his image to sell us everything from soap and diet beer to Japanese pickup trucks. If we can't live outdoors or ride free across the range, we can surely get a taste of the cowboy's life by smoking the right cigarette.

At the center of this pop culture storm is just an unschooled boy on a half-wild horse, kicking up dust in the middle of nowhere. And yet he was

something more. During his days on the open range, he participated in what seemed like a great adventure. While he was out rounding up someone else's cattle and driving them to market, the cowboy was building a legacy that would far outlast him. White, Black, or Mexican, he had an abiding sense of pride in himself and in his trade. Proof, should we need any, was captured by the photographers who drifted across the range taking pictures of grinning, puffed-up cowboys—for fifty cents apiece.

When he was a young man, Theodore Roosevelt worked as a cowboy for two years. He knew the hard reality of the cowboy's life; how to castrate a bull and chase strays for sixteen hours a day. But by the time he became the twenty-sixth president of the United States, he had fallen so completely under the spell of the cowboy's towering legend that he was known to wax rhapsodic from time to time. That suited the cowboy, and the country, just fine. In *Ranch Life and Hunting Trail* (188), Roosevelt summed up how Americans feel about the cowboy and, by association, how they feel about themselves:

To appreciate properly his fine, manly qualities, the wild rough rider of the plains should be seen in his own home. There he passes his days, there he does his life-work, there, when he meets death, he faces it as a he has faced many other evils, with quiet, uncomplaining fortitude. Brave, hospitable, hardy, and adventurous, he is the grim pioneer of our race; he prepares the way for civilization from before whose face he must himself disappear....He lives in the lonely lands where mighty rivers twist in long reaches between the barren bluffs; where the prairies stretch out into billowy plains of waving grass, girt only by the blue horizon, plains across whose wordless breadth he can steer his course for days and weeks and see neither man to speak to nor hill to break level; where the glory and the burning splendor of the sunsets kindle the blue vault of heaven and the level brown earth till they merge together in an ocean of flaming fire.

Credits

Permission to use the following excerpts is gratefully acknowledged: From John R. Craddock, "Songs the Cowboys Sing," *Texas and Southwestern Lore,* Publications of the Texas Folklore Society, Number VI, 1927. Hopalong Cassidy's Creed for American Boys and Girls and use of Hopalong Cassidy trademarks under license from U.S. Television Office, Inc., Reprinted by permission. All rights reserved.

Permission to use the following visual material is also gratefully acknowledged: All archival images used courtesy of the Twan Family archives, except pages 4 and 39 by Evelyn Maurice, and page 25 by J. Rosettis. The original oil paintings of Buffalo Bill on pages 18 and 19, and of the Earps on pages 78 and 79, reproduced by permission of the artist, Michael Downs. Use of the poster "Hopalong Cassidy Returns" on page 92 is authorized under License from U.S. Television Office, Inc., Copyright Owner. The postcard "Custer's Last Stand" on pages 56 and 57 is used courtesy of Buffalo Bill Historical Center, Cody, Wyoming. Reprinted by permission. All rights reserved.

Selected Bibliography

Adams, Ramon F. (ed.). *The Best of the American Cowboy.* Norman: University of Oklahoma Press, 1957.

Adams, Ramon F. *Western Words, A Dictionary of the American West.* Norman: University of Oklahoma Press, 1968.

Cannon, Hal (ed.). *Cowboy Poetry, A Gathering.* Salt Lake City: Gibbs M. Smith Inc., 1985.

Dary, David. *Cowboy Culture, A Saga of Five Centuries.* New York: Alfred A. Knopf, 1981.

Forbis, William H. *The Cowboys.* New York: Time-Life Books, 1973.

Frantz, Job B., and Julian Ernest Choate, Jr. *The American Cowboy, The Myth and the Reality.* Norman: University of Oklahoma Press, 1955.

Hough, Emerson. *The Story of the Cowboy.* New York: D. Appleton-Century Company, 1935.

Lomax, John A., and Alan Lomax. *Cowboy Songs and Other Frontier Ballads.* New York: The MacMillan Company, 1945.

O'Neil, Paul. *The End and the Myth,* Alexandria, VA: Time-Life Books, 1979.

Ward, Geoffrey C. *The West, An Illustrated History.* Boston: Little, Brown and Company, 1996.

TWO

THE TREASUR

2

THE

REPU

2

TWO

DOLLARS